HOW TO BE MARRIED

AN INSTRUCTION MANUAL
FOR NEWLYWEDS

By Martin Baxendale

© Copyright Martin Baxendale 2008

Published by Silent But Deadly
Publications, 21 Bisley Road,
Stroud, Glos., GL5 1HF

Printed in England by
Stoate & Bishop Printers Ltd,
Shaftesbury Industrial Centre,
Cheltenham, Glos. GL51 9NH

ISBN: 978-0-9550500-8-4

CONTENTS

INTRODUCTION

One of the most important aspects of marriage, and something that most married couples eventually get very good at, is the constant rowing.

In fact, to be honest, pretty much the whole <u>point</u> of getting married is so that you'll have someone to argue, squabble and row with for the rest of your life.

And since the most successful marriages are those where the couple are compatible, it'll help if you've found someone who enjoys arguing and rowing as much as you, about the same sort of things as you and in the same ways as you.

For example, it'll probably never work out if one of you likes to have a bit of a disagreement once a fortnight while the other wants to have a shouting match almost every day.

It's even less likely to last if one of you is very keen on rowing while the other isn't interested at all, constantly smoothing things over, going along with anything for a quiet life and generally behaving like a doormat.

A couple like that will struggle to get even the most basic and essential marital squabbles off the ground, and the more argumentative partner may well end up looking outside the marriage for his or her rows.

Worst of all is where <u>two</u> wimpy non-argumentative types get together and splice the knot. That's just a recipe for disaster, inevitably resulting in a totally row-less, hollow and meaningless travesty of a union that's going nowhere slowly and boringly; an endless cuddly-wuddly, kissy-wissy procession of tediously row-free, lovey-dovey days stretching sickeningly from altar to grave.

Ideally, both marriage partners should be equally happy to start and share a bloody good row on any subject, no matter how trivial, at the slightest excuse and at any time of day or night.

But you shouldn't expect to reach that level of rowing excellence straight away. It can take a lot of practice and generally only comes with prolonged marital experience.

So don't worry if at first your married squabbles are few and far between or not up to the all-out shouting, swearing, door-slamming and crockery-smashing standards of your longer-married friends and relatives.

You'll get there too, eventually. And with this invaluable instruction manual to help you develop and improve your marital rowing, you'll soon be arguing and squabbling incessantly with the best of them.

7

GETTING STARTED

With any luck, you'll have managed to get in at least <u>some</u> pre-marital quarrelling and rowing practice prior to the wedding.

For example, while you were dating and/or living together, when taking the pregnancy test, planning the special day, having second thoughts, discovering that your partner-to-be snogged someone else on their stag/hen night, having more second thoughts, and so on.

But if, for some inexplicable reason, you've managed to get this far without rowing at all, ever (<u>really</u>??!) and have absolutely no idea how to get started, then it may be helpful to observe how more experienced married couples do it.

Simply invite round couples you know who've been married for a long time, open a few bottles of wine, sit back and wait for them to kick off. Be sure to have pencils and paper handy so you can discreetly take notes about any particularly interesting squabbling methods, techniques and tactics they use. Better still, a hidden tape recorder or video camera will allow you to replay and study every little detail of their rowing at your leisure.

Experienced marital rowing partners can easily be snapping at one another after just one glass, and at each other's throats by the second bottle, without any help at all and for no apparent reason.

If you do need to speed things up, try leading the conversation towards potentially touchy subjects like money problems, having more children, past sexual infidelities, exactly how much they'd like to strangle each other, etc. That should do the trick.

But assuming that you do have at least <u>some</u> basic pre-marital amateur rowing experience, what should be your next step? Well, first you need to make sure you have the basic married couple's squabbling and rowing tool kit:

Door for slamming.

And another thing...

Short fuses.

Crockery for smashing.

Specially toughened fingers for angry chest-poking (keep nails long and painful, and toughen tips of fore-fingers by repeatedly jabbing them into bowls of wet sand, karate-style).

Audience: nosey neighbours listening on other side of wall.

Megaphone and/or home karaoke machine for shouting each other down (and to ensure nosey neighbours hear properly - you don't want them thinking you're not keeping up your marital rowing duties properly).

Scoreboard for keeping track of points scored and rows won and lost.

13

Next, you need to start working on acquiring and improving the basic skills and techniques that are essential for prolonged marital squabbling and full-scale married rowing.

These include (to name just a few): Nagging, needling, nit-picking, being sarcastic, criticising, point-scoring, finger-pointing, eyeball-rolling, foot-stamping, rude hand gestures, swearing, door-slamming, crockery-smashing, glaring, sighing, tutting, slagging off, poking fun, sneering, sniggering, twisting the truth, muttering under your breath, sulking, being resentful, holding grudges, never letting things go, making voodoo dolls of your partner, etc, etc.

If you haven't already developed some of these basic skills and techniques, now is the time to start. And if you have, then you'll still need to practice and hone them to the much higher levels of expertise required to meet the demands of married life and its endless quarrels and rows.

It will also help if at least one of you has plenty of <u>annoying</u> <u>habits</u> which will repeatedly get on the other's nerves day after day, week after week, year after year, constantly causing rows and squabbles.

If you're <u>both</u> blessed with a wide range of annoying and/or disgusting habits, so much the better. But if <u>neither</u> of you has any irritating little habits <u>at</u> <u>all</u>, now that you're married it's time to get some (see list of suggestions under 'How To Start Rows' on page 35).

In addition, at least one partner in the marriage should <u>snore</u> <u>loudly</u>.

Snoring every night will keep the other partner awake, making them sleep-deprived, constantly tired and ratty, so much more likely to always be in the mood for a row (having a baby has a similar effect, only much greater - see page 45).

Ideally you should <u>both</u> snore like walruses, so that you keep each other awake. If your partner snores but you don't, you can always fake it.

Keeping a row <u>diary</u> or <u>calendar</u> will help when it comes to finding time in your busy schedules to fit in all that squabbling and rowing you should be doing. Use it to plan your rows in advance and make sure they don't get squeezed out by less important marital stuff like talking, cuddling and having sex.

18

Now you're ready to start what will hopefully be a very long, happy life of marital rowing together, and no doubt you can't wait to get at it.

But remember, don't try to spend every minute of the day rowing at first, as much as you'd like to. Pace yourselves and build up to it slowly. Only the most experienced marital partners who have been together for many years find it easy to quarrel absolutely non-stop, with one row running seamlessly into another.

Take breaks to plan your next row, and if necessary don't hesitate to go back and repeat the same row again and again and again until you're sure you've got it right. Remember, practice makes perfect.

WHAT TO ROW ABOUT?

The simple answer is anything and everything, no matter how big or how trivial.

In fact, the more trivial the better because quarrelling about the big stuff is actually quite easy. The real skill is in starting and maintaining blazing rows about the tiniest things. Indeed, some of your best rows will probably be about incredibly unimportant stuff like which one of you put a teaspoon in the cutlery drawer the wrong way round.

To take something as minor as that and blow it up into a full scale shouting match, complete with door-slamming, crockery-smashing and furious teaspoon-bending, is an art form.

But while you're still learning, here are some of the more obvious choices to start with. Get in some practice with these, then you can try being more adventurous in your choice of subject matter.

<u>MONEY</u>: One of the top choices for a good marital row. Who wastes all the money? Who could cut back on what to help save money? Who earns more than who? Who <u>could</u> earn more if they pulled their bloody finger out? Etc, etc. Lots of excellent starting points for some really great long-running squabbles.

SEX: Absolutely brilliant topic for marital rows and quarrels! Really, really brilliant! Ask any experienced married couple.

Are you having enough? Are you having too much? Have you been having it with <u>someone</u> <u>else</u>? Does it last long enough? Did your ex do it better/more/longer than your marital partner? Did your ex do that thing your marital partner refuses point-blank to even think about? Is foreplay <u>really</u> essential? <u>Was</u> it an accident when you tried putting it in the wrong hole or did you do it on purpose? Whose turn is it to sleep on the wet patch? Porn - good/bad? The possibilities for superb x-rated rows are simply endless.

And the best thing of all about rows to do with sex is that the more you row about sex, the less likely you are to have it. Which makes you both grumpier and rattier and even more inclined to row about it and even less likely to have it...etc, etc.

Well we might have sex more often if your "foreplay" lasted more than 3 minutes... ...including the 2½ minutes it always takes you to find my clitoris!!
And you can turn that bloody video camera off too!!
SULK!
WHIRRR!

HOUSEWORK: Who does more housework than who (or who does <u>all</u> the housework and who does <u>none</u>) is yet another favourite rowing subject that will keep cropping up in almost every marriage.

The related issue of tidiness is also good for a few regular rows. Luckily, in most marriages one partner is always tidier (i.e. women) than the other partner (i.e. men). Until evolution finally endows all men with the ability to pick up their own socks and underpants, this will always be a perennial rowing favourite too.

No, that's the dishwasher, not the washing machine. Try again...

Oh come on, you'll enjoy a repeat of Sex And The City **much** more than some silly World Cup final!

CLICK!

WATCHING TV: Arguing about what to watch on TV is a marriage staple. Ideally you should only have one television in the house, as having more than one greatly reduces the opportunities for you to clash over your favourite programmes night after night.

Squabbling over who has the TV remote is an even bigger deal, though, and winning or losing this particular row has immense symbolic importance in a marriage. Remember, it's not just about changing channels - it's about <u>who's</u> <u>in</u> <u>control</u>.

25

TOILET SEAT: Leave it up or down? This one is another biggie in the marital rowing stakes, and one that many married couples never manage to settle amicably. So a great row to revisit time and time again - in fact every time the 'seat down' partner visits the loo and finds the seat up (or worse still, finds herself sitting on freezing cold porcelain).

Splashing is another, equally contentious, toilet issue that's guaranteed to cause continual friction and result in heated rows (especially if the 'seat down' partner finds herself sitting on freezing cold, _wet_ porcelain).

Did you super-glue the toilet seat down again?!!!

HOW TO START ROWS

There are many, many, many, many, many ways to start a row with your marriage partner.

Couples who've been married for a very long time will often develop an uncanny ability to start rowing quite spontaneously with no apparent reason or cause. One minute they'll be sitting quietly and the next they'll be going at it like cat and dog.

But to reach that almost mystical highest level of marital rowing skill takes many years of practice and Zen-like dedication. And even the most experienced of long-married couples need a little help sometimes. Beginners will need it even more.

So here are some of the most common and useful basic marital row-starting strategies. Use them wisely.

1) Regularly practice giving your marriage partner 'looks'. You know, the kind of looks that say far more than mere words. Derogatory looks, contemptuous looks, scornful looks, mocking, disdainful, pitying, derisive, and "how did I end up with you?" looks. All are incredibly effective at starting rows.

Did you just give me one of your looks?!!

No I bloody didn't!

Yes you bloody **did**!!!

So what if I did?!!

2) There are all kinds of provocative things you can drop into the conversation in the course of a minor disagreement to greatly increase the chances of it turning into a full-blown row.

For example, "Don't be so stupid", "Look, I'll explain it again more slowly", "Just listen and you might learn something", "You do talk rubbish", "Blah, blah, blah, blah, blah!", "Sorry, did you say something? I stopped listening five minutes ago", "You sound just like your mother", "Football's a stupid game", "If you were a real man...", etc, etc.

By trial and error, you'll eventually learn what out of all the needling things you say to your marital partner are the most likely to get him or her going. Note those things well. They are invaluable weapons in your row-starting arsenal.

3) Constantly interrupting your marital partner is also a good row-starting technique, and so is repeatedly finishing their sentences for them.

4) Muttering under your breath can also help get a row started. As in: "Mutter, mutter", "What did you

say?", "Nothing", "It **wasn't** nothing! What did you bloody **say**?!!", "Nothing", **"WHAT DID YOU F***ING SAY?!!"** etc, etc.

5) Continually disagreeing with and contradicting your partner is also good for kick-starting rows.

I want to have more sex!   No, you don't!

I want to go to the pub!   No you don't!

I'm going to top myself!   I'll get a rope...

6) Constantly criticising everything your partner does is guaranteed to spark off plenty of rows. If you can combine this with comparing your partner to former boyfriends/girlfriends, so much the better.

At least my ex could bloody **cook**!!

Yeah? Well **my** ex didn't have a willy that I needed a bloody magnifying glass to see!!

7) Blame your partner for everything that goes wrong, even when you know it's really your own fault (in fact especially when it's your own fault).

8) Tell your partner plenty of lies and make sure that you get found out. Lies that you get away with are no use for getting rows going. They have to be blatant lies that any fool could see through, and you must stick to your story no matter how ridiculous if you're to arouse the maximum irritation and provoke a really decent row. The aim should be to treat your partner like an idiot who's easily duped and can be fobbed off with the lamest of excuses.

9) Be as bossy as possible, always telling your marital partner what to do and insisting they do things your way.

10) Always forget important occasions like wedding anniversaries and birthdays. Traditionally this is the

role of the husband. **They're just better at it. But if you prefer, in the interests of equality, you can take turns.**

11) Being late all the time helps too. If you are going to be late, never ever phone to warn your partner.

33

12) Flirting with other people is a sure-fire way to get a row going with your partner. To be sure of a really good drunken quarrel on the way home from parties, make it as obvious as possible.

Oooh! You're gorgeous! Hic! D'you fancy a quick snog while my husband's in the toilet?...... He's right behind me, isn't he?

13) Annoying habits are great for sparking off rows when one of you, driven to the edge of sanity, ends up screaming "For the millionth sodding time, will you stop f***ing doing that!!!"

But one or two annoying habits aren't really enough to see you through those many long years of married life. So from the following suggestions choose a few more

annoying habits that you think you might have an aptitude for and would enjoy inflicting on your partner (some are covered in more detail on other pages):

Humming, finger-tapping, whistling, picking nose, farting loudly, belching loudly, clearing throat noisily and disgustingly, blowing nose ditto, picking teeth, eating with mouth wide open, slurping drinks, farting in bed, obsessive tidying (so your partner can never find anything), leaving toilet seat up, always finishing partner's sentences for him/her, always being late, flirting with other men/women, ogling other men/women, backseat driving, leaving top off toothpaste tube, always saying "I told you so", scratching balls and sniffing fingers, cutting toenails at the dinner table, farting at the dinner table, reading porn at the dinner table (if a lot of these sound like things only men would do, well duh!)

14) And finally, nagging. Once you've identified something your partner really, really doesn't want to do and has no intention of ever doing, that's the time to start nagging them about it. The point isn't to make them do it (you know that's never going to happen) but to repeatedly foment rows.

KEEPING ROWS GOING

How to keep your rows going as long as possible is an important marital skill and one that you need to learn right from the start.

Otherwise, you'll find yourselves continually wasting perfectly good rows with long-running potential by getting them over with far too quickly. Instead, learn to drag your rows out and keep them going for hours, days, weeks, months and even years.

Think of it like Tantric sex, where you make the sex last for ages and ages, prolonging the pleasure as much as possible - only with squabbles, quarrels, bickering and rows instead of, y'know, bumping hairy bits.

For a start, never ever admit you're in the wrong, even when it's blatantly obvious that you are. Never accept any blame for anything, even when you're clearly at fault. Just keep arguing stubbornly, ignore the facts, refuse to listen to your partner's side of things and never try to see anything from their point of view.

Never, ever, ever apologise. Or at least not sincerely. A sarcastic apology is fine and, rather than ending the row, will help keep it going very nicely (provided you make it <u>very</u> sarcastic - just a hint of sarcasm may not do the trick).

Oh I'm so **sorry**! Of **course** it's all **my** fault! Everything's **always** my fault isn't it?! I'm so **stupid**! I ought to change my name to 'Hey, stupid!' to make things easier for you...

You're really getting the hang of this sarcasm thing, aren't you?

Insisting on having the last word will also prolong a row provided you <u>both</u> insist on having the last word. In fact you can keep that game of verbal ping-pong going indefinitely.

If you do start to run out of steam, rather than ending the row it's much better to stall by going off into a sulk and refusing to talk, flouncing off in a huff or storming out and slamming the door.

This will keep things in the air until you've both had to time to regroup, consider new strategies, think of counter-arguments and points to score and are ready to pick it up again when you're fresh and rested.

Finally, if you're tempted to kiss and make up, don't. Never let the desire to have making-up sex over-ride keeping a good row going. If desperate, you can always have the sex while you're both still mad and quarrelling. Better that than bringing a really good row to a premature end just for the sake of some momentary sexual enjoyment. Trust me, you'll regret it.

WHERE AND WHEN TO ROW

After a bit of practice, married couples are usually happy rowing anywhere, anytime. But there are certain situations and times which are <u>ideally suited</u> to the development of a good row.

These are the times and places that you can hope to get your very best rows going, truly momentous and memorable screaming matches that you'll look back on with pride and a real sense of achievement and accomplishment. Any onlookers won't forget them in a hurry either.

Basically, those perfect times and places are when there'll be lots of booze around plus other people to flirt with and/or members of your respective families to get involved, poke their noses in and generally get on your nerves and greatly improve your chances of getting a jolly good row started.

Drunken nights out in pubs and bars are obviously good, especially if you've already started rowing before going out (as will often happen if one of you is very slow getting ready, tries to criticise what the other's decided to wear, etc).

Parties are excellent, of course - a dangerous mix of free-flowing booze, other pissed people to flirt with, plus music and dancing allowing you the opportunity to mock each other's performances on the dance floor (clubbing also works well for the same reasons).

Wow! You've got much nicer boobs than my wife! Hic!

Special occasions like anniversaries, birthdays, Valentine's Day, Christmas, etc are also very good, especially if you're already squabbling because one of you forgot the occasion, forgot to buy a present, bought a crap present, etc. And, again, there's generally booze around to lubricate the rows.

You gave me an **ironing board cover?!!!**

You gave me a **penis enlarger?!!!**

Equally good are boozy special occasions where relatives are invited, such as wedding receptions, wakes, family Christmases, and suchlike gatherings. Even simple Sunday lunches with family invited can be promising flash-points for marital rowing.

And last but by no means least a quick note for less experienced male marital partners: When your female partner has **PMT** is absolutely one of the <u>very</u> best times you can choose to start a row. But once you've lit the blue touch-paper, do make sure you retire to a safe distance, and for your own safety, try not to pour <u>too</u> <u>much</u> petrol on the flames.

Did you just ask me if I'm grumpy because I've got **PMT** ?!!! Do you have a bloody **DEATH WISH?!!!**

IF YOU'RE HAVING PROBLEMS

If after a while your marital rows start to get a bit predictable and boring, and you find that you're rowing less and not enjoying it so much, there are various steps you can take to spice things up and put the va-va-voom back into you rowing.

Step 1) Make videos of your rows, to watch later. This will help you to spot ways you can improve your rowing techniques. Watching yourselves in action will also tend to get you going again, stimulating you into re-starting old rows and enjoying them all over again. Va-va-voom!

Step 2) Have a bit-on-the-side. Nothing will get you rowing again faster than one of you getting caught having a bit-on-the-side. But be warned, it may propel you straight to Step 6) Divorce proceedings, which is great for rowing but you may want to try some other things first.

Okay, yes I have been seeing another woman. But we only had a row **once**, and I was thinking of **you** the whole time!

Step 3) Decide to have a baby. New baby = sleepless nights and tired, ratty mum and dad = lots more rows (especially about who's not doing their fair share of looking after baby) plus new baby = lots of expensive baby stuff to buy = lots more rows about money. Brill!

As a bonus, before the new baby arrives with all the row-enhancing sleepless nights and expense, there's the <u>pregnancy</u>. Also a pretty good time for rows.

I'm constantly tired, my back aches, my legs are swollen, my breasts hurt, I've got morning sickness, the baby's kicking me.....and you want me to **iron your sodding shirt?!!!**

KICK!

Step 4) If you already have children by the time you start to experience problems with your rowing, then take them on a family holiday. Yet another good time for marital rows, which starts with the packing and just gets better and better as more things go wrong.

Step 5) Go to Marriage Counselling. Fantastic chance to re-visit and re-fight every row you've ever had...

Step 6) If counselling doesn't help get you rowing again, then you can always start divorce proceedings. That's when the arguments <u>really</u> hot up.

Step 7) Of course, you can always just wait until old age sets in. Then you'll forget that you've had all the rows you've been through over the years and be able to have them all over again, and again, and again, and again, and again....

<u>ALSO AVAILABLE</u> (by Martin Baxendale)....